CHILDHOOD
MEMORIES
OF
SHINBONE
VALLEY

DEDICATION

This little book is dedicated to Thomas Charles Jordan, the namesake of Thomas Wayne Harwell. Born December 3, 2018 to Madelyn Elizabeth Smith Jordan and Zachary Scott Jordan. Little Thomas is the great grandson of Thomas and Marcelle Harwell and grandson of Lori Bartran Howell.

This honor has brought great joy to Thomas, his great grandfather. His desire is that Thomas will carry this name with pride, being that it is carried down seven generations, since Thomas Payne Strickland in 1855. A man that brought honor to his ancestors in his mountain home of Shinbone Valley, Alabama, in the Appalachian Mountains. A name of Noble Scottish ancestry.

Thomas Charles Jordan, named after his Great Grandfather Thomas Wayne Harwell

ACKNOWLEDGEMENTS

I would like to thank the members of Shinbone Valley for their help in sharing family pictures, genealogy and beautiful scenic views of the mountains and valleys of the Appalachian Mountains.

Strickland descendants have been very kind in their willingness to share their family history. I would like to name the ones who have been most helpful. Ruby Faye Johnston, Marsha Strickland Conville and Donald Strickland. All have been a wealth of family history.

Also, I want to thank Michele Sims Payne for information on the Payne bloodline.

Angela Morgan can not be left out of our appreciation of her sharing the beautiful scenery of Alabama and the majesty of its beauty by her photography. Her extensive travels all through the forest, valleys, mountains and streams, has brought to life the real natural wonder of this almost unknown splendor of the Appalachian Mountain region.

Donald Strickland deserves a special thank you for welcoming his unknown cousin, Tom, to stay in his cabin and the personal scenic tour of Tom's great, great grandfather, Ancel Butler Strickland's old home site and the grounds he played on as a child. Chief Shinbone's burial site was an added plus, along with the granite marker in the Chiefs honor.

Also, I would like to mention, Vista Strickland's little book about her life in Shinbone Valley. It was an inspiration to me in writing my husband's childhood memories. She brought to life everyday life in a place virtually unknown and hidden from most of the world. Her words echoed what my husband shared with me, plus so much more.

From the bottom of my heart I want to express my gratitude and sincere thanks. Without all of the above people and their help, this little book, Childhood Memories of Shinbone Valley, would not be what it is.

Thomas Wayne Payne Harwell feels a kindred spirit to all of you that opened your mind and hearts to him. Because of this he is able to leave behind his story of the valley he loved in the sunset of his life.

Mountains on the Appalachia and the Valley below.

PROLOGUE

The true-life story of an unwanted new born baby boy, that was given away at one week old.

Born to an unwed mother, raised in Ohatchee, Alabama, and her mother being a poor widow with too many children to care for, insisted her daughter give the baby away. The adoption was posted in a tiny article in the Anniston Star Newspaper.

A young, newly married girl saw the small advertisement and she and her husband adopted the fine baby boy.

Here in these pages are the childhood experiences from the memories of a boy they called Tommy.

Now, seventy-eight years old, the telling of his story is very dear to his heart. The most cherished of all of his memories, being the summers spent in Shinbone Valley, Alabama.

A secret valley, hidden away from the modern civilization; seemingly where time had passed it by. Living there, as if they were still in the 1800s. A place of untouched beauty in the valley of the Appalachian Mountains.

CHAPTERS

THE ANNISTON STAR, JUNE 9TH, 1940, SUNDAY

The Anniston Star
ANNISTON, ALA., SUNDAY, JUNE 9, 1940.

Stare Legislature Will Meet Monday For Speedy Action

PLAN IS READY UPON REARMING OF THIS NATION

French Army Retreats Before German Drive

GERMAN PLANES HIT AT ENGLAND IN NIGHT RAIDS

Anniston Star "War Reporter" Makes "Strategic Withdrawal"

BUSINESS RECEIVES ADDED MOMENTUM

Adoption Add

CHAPTER I
GIVEN AWAY

June 9th, 1940, a tiny 1" x 2" ad was placed in the personal section of the Anniston Star Newspaper, Anniston, Alabama. It read, '6 1/2 lb. Baby Boy, one week old for adoption. Will sign adoption papers. Applicants must be able to furnish good references. State your income. Write X.Y.Z., care Anniston Star.'

This yellow, tattered edge old newspaper from 1940 was a heartbreaking site. As one scans the pages of this paper, the headlines of the day were tragic enough. World War II was raging in Europe. 'The French Army Retreats before German Drive.' 'German Planes hit at England in Night Raids.' "General Pershing Urges Unlimited Supplies to the Allied Armies.' With the world in chaos, a new-born comes into the world un-welcome. Americans will fight till the death for our Freedom and the Freedom of the innocent victims of tyranny and yet an innocent little baby is born to poverty and shame and must be turned away.

He came into this world on May 27, 1940, on the graduation night of his young mother. She went into labor at her graduation commencements, and her sisters rushed her home. The doctor was called, and she gave birth without complications. As she looked into the face of this tiny baby boy, she could see he looked so much like her baby pictures. She began to cry knowing she would have to give him up. She was heartbroken and ashamed of what she was putting her family through. The disgrace was hard to bear. She refused to say who the father was. This is a secret she took to her grave!

Her two sisters, Orlis and Nola, fell in love with him at first site. It was a heartbreaking choice that he had to be given up. One of her sisters in a last show of love made the precious baby boy a blue crochet blanket to wrap him in as he was taken from his mother, to never see him again. It had to be one of the most difficult things she ever had to do in her life.

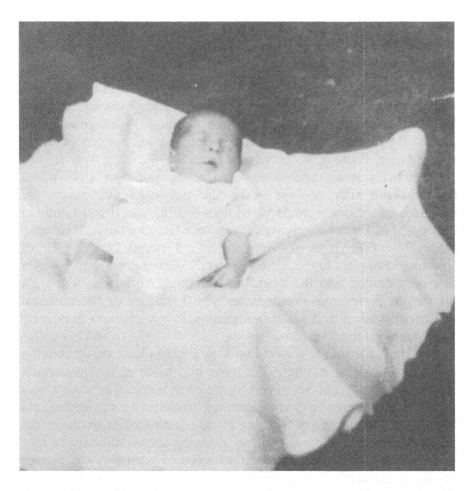

First picture taken of Wayne Payne, aka Thomas Wayne Harwell; two weeks old.

Little Tommy, age 6 months

A short time later Naomi would marry. One supposes her new husband was not aware of the baby she had given up only months before. He was in the Army and went to the Panama Canal Zone, so, what was known by some was never divulged to him.

Many years later after this baby was a grown man his daughter would research and find his biological mother. Before giving him up she named him, Wayne Payne. His new mother named him Thomas Wayne Harwell, after her grandfather, Thomas. Ironically his middle name was Payne. So far, a family connection has not been made. Tommy, as he was called all of his youth, did not learn of his adoption until he was grown. When he was about forty his real mother was discovered living only a short distance from where he was raised. However, when she was contacted, she did not want to see him. Her parents were both dead and also her husband. So, the mystery continues to haunt Thomas. Why would she not want to meet and get to know her only son? What could have been so bad that she couldn't face him? Now it's too late for answers, they are all gone that might have known.

Apparently, the Payne's have Native American heritage. Cherokee, from Cherokee, Georgia, was discovered in genealogy research done by Teresa Holloway, my daughter in law, who herself is of Indian distraction and is rather good at finding ancestors. It has been traced back to the 1780's. However, a very strange fact is that the Payne name appears to be a given name and not a surname. Regardless, it has been passed down for around two hundred and forty years.

Naomi Payne was obviously of Native American blood, because of her appearance. This passed to her illegitimate son, Wayne Payne, Tommy. Thomas Wayne Harwell.

The following is his genealogy from the Payne side.

PAYNE GENEALOGY

PETER RENFROE	married	MARGARET SPARKS
Cherokee, Co GA		Cherokee Co, GA

Daughter. Margaret Payne...B. 1809
married William Wiley Hood...B. 1809
(Children by this marriage were given the name Payne and Hood;
Margaret Sparks gave her daughter the name Payne, instead of her married name)
Larkin B. Payne...B. 1835

Martha Payne...B. 1937
Mary Payne...B. 1839
George W. Payne...B. 1840
James Paul Hood...B. 1844
Marion D. Hood...B. 1846
John Smith Hood...B. 1849
Milly A. Hood...B. 1852

Son. Larkin Berry Payne...B. 1835...D.1894
in Etowah, AL, in 1854 Married Elizabeth B. Coker...B. 1836
Children:
William Washington Payne...B. 1857
Margaret Payne...B. 1860
Georgia Payne...B. 1861
Mattie Payne...B. 1865
James Joseph Payne...B. 1867
John Payne...B. 1869
Marion D. Payne...B. 1873
Larkin B. Payne...B. 1875
Jackson Columbus Payne...B. 1879

Son: George Washington...B. 1857...D. 1905; born in Cherokee, GA, Lived in Etowah, AL.
Married Mary Etta Simpson; father, Alden Simpson; mother, Mary Melinda Walden.

Children: (7)
George Robert Marion
Larkin Hilman
Martha
Mary
John
Jane
Millie

Son: Hilman Larkin Payne...B. 1888...D. 1931
Married: Jane Magnolia Little...B. 1900

Children: (8)
Naomi
Orlis
Magnolia (Nola)
Grady...D. 1943; 15yrs old.; had Down Syndrome)
"Pete" LeeRoy

Clara
John Clemens
Mary Lamana
■■■
Daughter: Naomi Payne Stedman…B. 1922…D. 2004
Children:
Wayne Payne…B. 1940 (out of wedlock); Father unknown
Naomi Married: Stedman…D. 1941
Children: Annette Stedman…B.1942…D.
Joyce Stedman…B. 1943

****

For reasons unknown, she persisted in her refusal to never see her only son. After many years passed, she became ill and was on her death bed. As she lay dying her only living daughter, and half sister to Tommy, knew something was unfinished with her mother. She asked if it had something to do with her son, she apparently nodded, so she knew she wanted to hear his voice. Upon calling Tommy and asking if he would say something to her before she died, he agreed.

As we know this is a man that lived twenty years of his life knowing he was adopted and that he had a real mother that gave him up and after learning where he was refused to ever speak his name, tell him she was sorry and tell him she loved him. At that moment, the person on the other end of that telephone line knew Tommy had to have been endowed with love and forgiveness beyond her understanding. A character she lacked!

He told her everything was alright! He lied! His words were, "Naomi, every things okay."

One hopes she found peace, because she passed shortly after.

All of those years carrying that empty space in his heart, not ever knowing why she gave him away. Then, upon learning of her whereabouts, she showed no sign that she ever loved him. One can only know so much about a person's heart. The pain and hurt deep inside, that was kept from everyone. Even if this did not break his heart, it broke mine for him, as the wife that loves him and knows how much he loves his family. One can only pray and hope the mother who made that choice to adopt that sweet baby boy that she found advertised in a tiny ad in the newspaper; the one who gave him love and security was enough to heal that hurt.

Now 78 years old, he never speaks of the one who chose to forget him. Or, who his real father was.

So many memories never made, so many secrets taken to the grave!

Naomi Payne and her husband Forest Stedham

CHAPTER II
DORIS STRICKLAND

A twenty-year-old girl from Shinbone Valley, Alabama, married a man twice her age. Doris Strickland, an illegitimate young woman, who carried her mother's maiden name because she never knew who her father was saw a tiny advertisement about another fatherless child. It tugged at her heart and reminded her of growing up and never knowing a father.

Being sneered at and hearing ugly whispered remarks all of her youth. Doris had only been married a short time, not knowing if indeed she could have children of her own by a thirty-nine-year-old man. Of course, after seeing the newspaper it didn't matter to her, she wanted to give that unwanted baby a loving mother. Doris had all but raised her five sisters and one brother, because of her mother's questionable motherly instincts. So, she answered the ad and she and her husband, Theodore, met with the lawyer. The adoption was agreed upon and the papers signed. Doris and Theo took their new baby boy home. Naomi was not there to give the baby to his new mother. The doctor gave them the infant.

So thrilled about her baby, she shared the news with her family. They all loved him immediately. So tiny and beautiful. He was a good baby too. Sweet and happy. As though he knew he was going to be loved.

He had been given a name by his biological mother, of Wayne Payne, Payne being her maiden name. Doris wanted to name him after the only father she knew growing up, her grandfather, Thomas Payne Strickland. So, she named him Thomas and kept Wayne as he middle name. Thomas Wayne Harwell, and he was called Tommy. Why she kept Wayne in his name, we don't know. Maybe she felt the heartbreak of his eighteen-year-old mother who had to give him up. However, we don't think Naomi ever knew she did that.

Tommy's new father was very pleased too. Theo was a good hard-working, big hearted man. Six foot, four, he was above average in height of men at that time. However, Doris was tall as well, five foot ten inches.

Tommy's first birthday. His mother, Doris holding him; 1941

Home life in Anniston, Alabama was good for the most part. Tommy knew he was loved by both his adoptive parents. Of course, he would not be told until he was grown and out of the house about being adopted. An agreement made at the adoption.

Theo worked until retirement for Alabama Power, never being out of work even during the Great Depression. Doris worked at a ribbon factory. Tommy had a Mammie until he was old enough to take care of himself. He loved that big ole, sweet, black woman and she loved him.

Sadly, his father had a drinking problem, which caused some hardship for Tommy and his mother. His daddy would give away most of his pay check to poor folks before he ever got home with it. Doris would naturally be angry. Once Tommy was grown, they divorced. By this time Theo's health was very poor and he died a few years later with Tommy taking care of him.

STRICKLAND GENELOGY

Sir Roger Strickland…B. 1588 in England-Castle
Children:
Son: Soloman…D. 1626; Battle of Cow Pins, King MT, Carolina
Fought in American Revolution

Son: Ezekiel Morton…B. 1774, NC…D. 1818 Madison, CA; State Senator 1838, GA; married Jane Haynes

Son: Elisha…B. 1797, Morgan Co.,GA…D. 1861-1869 in Clay Co. AL; Barton's Co. Indian War; Married Mary Ann Holly

Son: Ancel Butler Strickland…B. 1816; Civil War Home Guard; 2nd Sergeant of John Hurst's Co.; Talladega Co. Reserves; married Agnes; four children
Married Agnes Rebecca Spruell; eleven children
Married Sarah Panel; six children

Son: Thomas Payne Strickland…B. 1855…D. 1940
Married: Elizabeth Susan Bruce "Lizzy"…B. 1862…D. 1951
Children: Walter, Zeck, Alvin, George; Annie, Delcie (handicap)

Annie Strickland…B. 1905; Shinbone Valley

Daughter: Dorris…B. out of wedlock, father unknown…B. 1920
Married: Joseph Brown
Children: Norris, Shirley, Inez, Lilly, Mary, Joann

Daughter: Doris Strickland Harwell...B. 1920
Married: Theodore Roosevelt...B. 1900
Adopted: Wayne Payne aka Thomas Wayne Harwell...B. 1940

Tommy; age three

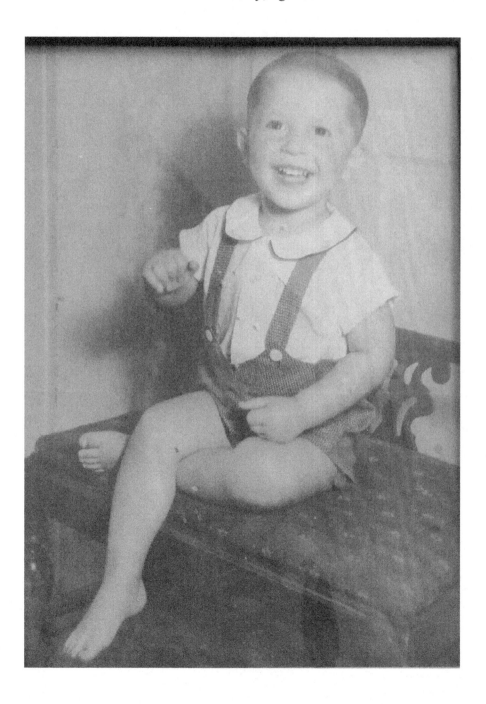

In the Valley of the Appalachian Mountains of Alabama was a wonderful adventure for Tommy as a child. Starting at a young age he would set out for the forest near his home of Anniston, Alabama. With a peanut butter sandwich in wax paper stuffed in his pocket, off he would go all alone to explore the woods. He loved nature and God's little creatures. Maybe his native American nature was coming out. As an adult those years were the best memories of his childhood.

That and the summers he spent at his grandmothers, Annie Strickland Brown's little mountain cabin in Shinbone Valley. These memories are his most cherished. These were poor mountain people in material possessions, but rich in the important things of life. Love of family and the simple pleasures that they carved out of this rough life they lived in. A little two room log and plank sided cabin with two chimneys for heat and cooking. Water from a nearby spring and fresh vegetables and meat from the land they owned. Chickens, a couple of cows, sheep, pigs and a good hunting dog or two was all anyone needed in this land of mountains, valleys, meadows, creeks and forest as thick and tall as the clouds. A paradise for anyone willing to work the land, build a home and take care of one's family and kin.

This existence has been going on as long as the white settlers came there. Mostly English and Scottish blood; they found these hidden valley's and the vast expanse of the Appalachians in the Southern lands of the Native American Tribes. Living together in harmony until they wanted all the land as more and more settlers came.

Finally, the government sent in soldiers to resettle the Native Indians to a land far away from their home. To a hostile land of waste and desolation in Oklahoma. This has gone down in history as "The Trail of Tears". Thousands died along the 2000-mile track, mostly their weak, old and children.

CHAPTER III
LAND OF THE INDIANS AND THEIR HISTORY

The Creek or Muskogee Confederacy had been in the South Eastern Region of America for several hundred years before white settlors. Once the most powerful tribe in the Southeast. Known as the Gulf Family/Muskogean Branch now called the Porch Band of the Creek nation. Their language was Muskogean. They are one of the five civilized tribes in America. Others are, Cherokee, Chickasaw, Choctaw and Seminole.

Their clans are: Wind, Bird, Alligator and Bear.

Clans traced their heritage from the female line. Never marrying in their clan. (This is the main reason so much mutation of bloodlines is happening among the tribes in Oklahoma today. The oral history of clans was kept by the elders and thousands died on the "Trail of Tears", taking that knowledge with them. They are marrying within their clans, causing horrible birth defects.)

One of the tragedies of Indian lands being taken from them was from one of their own Chief McIntosh, half Indian and half Scot betrayed his own people for monetary gain, while negotiating the Treaty of Indian Springs in 1825. The Creek Nation executed him and burned all of his properties.

The first known contact with white men started when Hernando Desoto made contact in 1540. This, as we know, went badly from thereafter, as more and more white men came to settle on their lands.

The land had been inhabited by Creeks, Cherokees and other tribes for hundreds of years, then to be driven from their homes was probably one of the worst crimes against humanity done in American history. The Native Americans to this day despise Andrew Jackson for ordering them driven from their homes to Oklahoma. The paradise they called home in the Appalachians was all they ever knew. I can't imagine the sorrow they knew and experienced.

Some hid in the great forests and mountains and escaped "The Trail of Tears". It is no wonder when the Scots or Ulster-Scots, came to this land of beauty and splendor in the late 1700s, that it suited them well, remembering the once tree covered mountains of home, the flowing brooks, the picturesque landscape of mountains and forest as far as the eye could see. The climate was even more pleasant than home. It is no doubt they fell in love with this land of beauty and plenty and wanted to claim it as their own.

As decades passed, the Ulster-Scots had no interest in progress and because of their isolation they were happily ignorant in their bliss.

Before the Civil War, they were much the same as many rural areas, but following the war they maintained their frontier characteristics. Which appears they were satisfied with their way of life.

However, the outside world considered them, "Hillbillies", ignorant, inbred and sometimes of a violent nature. Probably because of feuding families, like the Hatfield's and McCoy's.

Whatever status they got I doubt they really cared, as long as outsiders left them alone to just live their life in peace.

Typical appearance of a Creek Indian Chief

NATIVE AMERICAN BATTLES:

History tells us battles were fought with the normally peaceful Indians of Alabama's Appalachian Mountain area. White settlors began stealing Indian maidens from villages which caused a major conflict. Many Indians were massacred during this time.

During this period the Battle of Horseshoe Bend took place. A fierce Indian War in which Talladega County experienced one of the bloodiest battles in history. Shinbone Valley was encompassed in this horrific event and Davy Crockett was in the middle of it too. The war was fought against the Red Sticks, a part of the upper Creek nation, who were against their lands being taken. The opposing side was Andrew Jackson, Americans and allied Indians, the lower Creek, Cherokee and Choctaws. The end was a catastrophe for the upper Creek nation. Thus, ending the Creek War.

Sam Houston was also a third Lieutenant in the battle, receiving an arrow wound. The year was 1814. This was when Chief Shinbone was stripped of his title of Chief. A broken old man and his small family was left to the mercy of the "Favoring Winds".

Indian Warrior

CHAPTER IV
HISTORY OF THE STRICKLANDS

What many didn't know was a great number of these settlers came to America from noble backgrounds.

The Strickland's were among those, from England and Scotland nobility.

Starting with Sir Roger Strickland. Born in 1588, his son, Matthew, born in 1637 in England, but died in Virginia in 1719. Matthew II was born in 1659, but also died in Virginia in 1730. Son, Jacob was born in 1714 and died in 1818 in North Carolina. He was a Patriot in the American Revolution. His son, Solomon, born in 1735 died in 1818 in Georgia and fought at the Battle of Kings Mountain, probably knew my ancestors, Herndon and Rice, in the American Revolution. His son, Ezekiel, was a state senator in Georgia in 1838. Elisha, born in 1797 in Alabama, was a soldier in the War of 1812. Then his son Ancel B. Strickland, born in 1815 was home guard in the Civil War as a Sargent in John Hurst's Company. He died at Shinbone Valley in 1897. His second wife Rebecca Spruill was born in 1822 and died in 1870. Thomas Payne was the son of Ancel and Rebecca. Tommy's name-sake and his mother's grandfather.

Ancel B. Strickland came to Shinbone Valley years later from Georgia. Ancel built a fine home compared to the humble cabins scattered in the valley.

They say it was large enough for a live-in teacher/tutor for his many children, plus two farm hands lived there as well. He had stables for horses and livestock, lovely orchards and even flower beds in the front of his home with stone covered paths. Beautiful lily trees (Japanese Magnolias), black walnuts and an ancient red oak, that shaded the whole yard of clean swept clay.

It was said that Ancel was a handsome, tall figure of a man, with dark red curly hair and baby blue eyes. He had been widowed recently by his first wife, Agnes, who died young in childbirth. The newborn died as well. However, she gave him three children before her death at twenty-eight, two sons and a daughter.

Ancel Butler Strickland; Born 1816; Died 1897
Shinbone Valley, Alabama

Coming to the valley filled with grief and three children in tow, he soon forgot sorrow staying busy building his home. He came in about 1844, just after Agnes' death. He met Rebecca soon after and they married, some say she was Chief Shinbone's only daughter. If indeed, she was Chief Shinbone's daughter, which we don't know that for a fact, because she was said to be from South Carolina. Of course, from her pictures she certainly could pass for a Native American. We will probably never know for sure. She would have been twenty-two when he married her, and she gave him eleven more children. Including, Thomas Payne Strickland. Sadly, she would die at age forty-eight.

Ancel would outlive a third wife, Sarah Panel, and father twenty-one children, all together. He died in 1897 at his home in Shinbone Valley, and was buried at Union Cemetery in Clay County, Alabama. He was eighty-one.

Ancel Butler Strickland has gone down in history for his kindness to one of the last Chiefs of the Creek Nation. At least two other books have been written that include his honorable deed and well-respected life. Vista Strickland wrote a wonderful account of life in Shinbone Valley and the Strickland's.

Another note worthy fact about Ancel, is that he built a honeymoon home for his newly married children. Each couple, after their wedding ceremony would go to their little cabin and stay there until the young groom could build his bride a home of their own. Land was given to each and everyone of Ancel's children to build a home. This tradition continued till all of Ancel's many children married.

In later years after Ancel had passed on, one of his grandchildren lived in the honeymoon cabin. Sadly, today Ancel's fine home and the cabin are no longer standing, after over one hundred years.

Despite that Ancel Butler Strickland and his legacy will live on in the minds and hearts of his many descendants.

Ancel Butler Strickland and Agnes Rebecca Spruell; Wedding Picture

Rebecca Spruil and Ancel Butler Strickland with Thomas Payne Strickland

Typical cabin and farm

Doris Strickland Harwell's great grandfather was granted thousands of acres of land in Shinbone Valley, once belonging to Chief Shinbone. Ancel Butler Strickland was a good, honest and admirable man. Upon seeing what was being done to the Native Americans it was heartbreaking. Old Chief Shinbone and his clan were being hunted down to be driven from the only home his people had ever known. Ancel sought out the old Chief and his people and hid them away in the forest on his newly given land. They were spared the death march and resettlement and lived out their lives in what was named after him, Shinbone Valley. Ancel built Chief Shinbone a cabin and for this he was given a treasured possession of the Chief, his peace pipe. It is still one the families prized possessions to this day. When the Chief died, he was buried on the side of the mountain and a memorial stands in his memory.

Nothing had been said until now of the Chief's clan, the Creek Indians, marrying one of the Strickland's, but I have been informed by Donald Strickland, also great-grandson of Ancel Butler Strickland and his father Renzo, son of Clay, brother of Thomas Payne, that either Elisha Strickland or Ancel married Chief Shinbone's daughter. I believe it is a strong possibility it was Rebecca Spruill because of the description of her from over a hundred years ago. It said, "she had dark hair and eyes and a kind face". If this is true, Thomas Payne, being her son, would be half Creek Indian.

Memorial of Chief Shinbone; Chief of the Creek Indians of Clay County Alabama.

Donald lives in Shinbone Valley on a part of the original Strickland land, 350 acres of what was once several thousand acres. He lives in the house built by his grandfather Clay Strickland. Donald is 80 years young. I say this because after talking to him for the first time for over two hours, I learned some interesting facts. Ancel and Rebecca married in 1844 and the Creek Indian Removal Act began in 1838. It has also been said, when they met, she was 22 and he was 29. Obviously, they became like family because of the Chief giving him his peace pipe.

Clay Strickland; Donald Strickland's Grandfather

Of course, we have no real proof of Rebecca being Chief Shinbone's daughter. Ancel came to Alabama a grieving widower, with three children. It is quite certain he needed a wife to help him raise his family. There is no record of how Rebecca got to that particular location, being that she supposedly came from South Carolina. All of the pieces fit for her to be the Chief's daughter and a match being made between Ancel and the Chief because of Ancel saving their lives. A gift of a Chief's most prized possession, his daughter would be logical as this is how Native Americans showed gratitude and favor.

If in deed, this is true, the match seemed to be a good one for all concerned. Rebecca gave Ancel eleven children. The fine home he built her was also a sign of love for the Indian maiden he married.

Tommy's mother comes from this union of love.

Thomas Payne Strickland, son of Ancel and Rebecca, married Elizabeth Bruce, "Lizzie". Their six children were Annie, Delcie (crippled), Walter, George, Alvin and Zeck.

Thomas built a nice home for his family. Having one really large room, plus a kitchen and it had an upstairs for bed rooms, reached by a ladder. Two huge fireplaces in each downstairs room. I assume the four sons slept upstairs.

Tom also had a gristmill on his place. He was an industrious and hard-working man like his father before him.

Doris, his granddaughter, by Annie, adored him. He was the only father she ever knew. He was very kind and loving to his little fiery, red headed granddaughter. From the beginning of her childhood he knew she wasn't going to take any nonsense from anyone. He loved her spunk and tenacity. Doris was probably fortunate that she was raised by them. She received more attention and love than in a household full of children. She did turn out to be like a mother to her half sisters and brother. At different times one or the other lived with her and Theo in Anniston. She wasn't an affectionate person, but she would do anything for those she loved and her kin.

Her life in Shinbone Valley was one of cherished memories. Very likely why she wanted Tommy to experience it as well. Not so much because of her mother, Annie, living there, but the valley itself. There are few places on God's earth that compare to the beauty and harmony of nature in that place of natural wonder. Furthermore, she wanted him to really get to know her siblings.

Gristmill similar to Thomas Payne Strickland's

Back row from the left, Annie Strickland, Walter, George, Alvie and Zeck Bottom from left, Thomas Payne Strickland, Delcie(crippled) & wife Elizabeth (Lizzie) Bruce

Son, George, wife, Lizzie and Thomas Payne Strickland

Tommy loved all of them. He played with the younger girls and followed Norris around like a puppy. Norris enjoyed every minute of it. Being that he and Tommy were the only males there.

This is where the blood of the Strickland's come from. Good strong people endowed with honor and God-fearing morals. Mountain life was harsh, only the strong survived. Even though Tom doesn't have that blood flowing in his veins, he was fortunate to be raised by these poor but proud people. I say poor, only in the sense of worldly possessions, not poor in spirit. Of course, this hard life was not suited for just anyone. However, it seemed to be a haven to folks of this natural predisposition and passion.

CHAPTER V
ANNIE STRICKLAND BROWN

Doris being born out of wedlock, when Annie, her mother, was quite young. Her father and mother, Thomas and Lizzy, raised Doris. When Annie got married to Mr. Brown, Doris stayed on at her grandparents' cabin until she was grown. So, in truth, Doris was never raised or thought of Annie, as her mother. She loved her grandfather dearly, so she named her adopted son after him.

Supposedly, she never had any idea who her father was. I am sure much speculation arose when it was discovered she was with child. Annie's father, Thomas, had to be very angry that someone would take his young daughter, whether by persuasion or force. That was a dangerous thing in those times. There had been occasions of shot gun weddings or even worse, someone was killed for shaming a young girl. Apparently, the father was someone known and could not be forced to marry Annie, for the shear shame on the family.

Thomas came from honorable ancestors and it was known far and wide what kind of man his father, Ancel was. This had to have been very difficult for him. The shame and humiliation were probably one of great pain.

Annie took a husband a short time after Doris was born. Brown built her a cabin on land given them by her father. She had eight children by him. Seven daughters and one son.
Brown was a good Christian man, and well thought of in the valley. He helped build the Union Church and did other good Christian deeds.

He must have died fairly young because he had been passed sometime when Tommy went to visit, maybe five or six years.

Her son Norris was the only man on the place being that her husband and father had both passed away. The burden of mans work fell on his shoulders. With a crippled arm, he did quite well in keeping the farm going. A kind and humble person, Tommy thought the world of Norris.

Norris built his own house on the hill just up from Annie's place. He had married a pretty young Cherokee Indian girl, named Esther.

Cabin and farm, similar to Annie Brown's; the springs were in the back, down the hill and back up again. The mountains could be seen all around.

Thomas, or Tommy as he was called as a child, spent many wonderful summers in Shinbone Valley at his adopted mother's, mothers home, Annie Strickland Brown. When Tommy's mother was born to Annie Strickland, she was unmarried, so Doris kept her mother's maiden name. Doris would take Tommy to visit her during the summer and leave him with Annie and her children by her husband, Brown, then deceased. His childhood memories are his most endearing at this time in his life.

The old house was two rooms, two fireplaces and a porch. Partly logs and old rough unpainted board siding with stone fireplaces. One mostly for heat, while the other for cooking. She did have a wood burning stove that she used for baking breads and pies. There was one feather bed in the main room for all the children and a small cot against the wall for Annie. A table for eating was in the kitchen room with a prepping table and pie safe. Water was brought from the spring in buckets for cooking, washing and bathing. Bath time was once a week, in front of the fireplace in winter. The water was heated from the stove, but in winter it was still very cold. The baby and youngest got a bath first and older children last. By that time, I imagine the water wasn't very clean. Hygiene wasn't the most important thing, because getting a fever, colds, flus and the like could be deadly without medical accessibility.

Speaking of this, Shinbone Valley was very remote and isolated. Just to go to the nearest general store was a real outing for the family and would take all day there and back. Pyriton, Alabama was the nearest, having a general mercantile store, black smith, post office, church, train station, gristmill and a few homes. What a thrill it was for all the young ones. This trip was taken by a mule and wagon. Rough Indian trails and foreboding streams was the only road to any kind of civilization. The closest doctor or hospital was over forty miles away, so any sickness, accidents or birthing babies were taken care of by healers or mid-wives. This would usually be a woman who had the gift of healing and knowledge of roots and herbs that had healing powers. This "gift" was passed down through the generations in certain families.

CHAPTER VI
TOMMY'S FIRST VISIT TO SHINBONE VALLEY

Beginning at the age of seven Tommy went on his first visit to Grandma Annie's in Shinbone Valley. So excited when they got off the main road and began the journey to a place that appeared to be hidden in the dense forest. Down little narrow dirt roads sunken into the earth by thousands of years of Indian trails. The giant trees of virgin pine, hickory, oak, popular and walnuts towering high above the earthen sides of the ancient roads taken by many an Indian Brave in days gone by. The coolness of the air and the sweet smells of honey suckle filled Tommy's nostrils. The sounds of the forest with birds chirping and crickets rubbing their legs together, gave him a churn in his stomach and the excitement that lay ahead.

The road changed as the old ford car made its way up the side of Cheatta Mountain. The beauty higher up was something to behold. Valleys and creeks lay below. Tree covered mountains as far as the eye could see. God's beauty showed out as lazy clouds floated by in the blue sky. Now they were going down the mountain into the valley, not a car or person in sight. It was like Tommy was going across some great divide that separated civilization with its roads, houses, town lights, noisy streets and cars going everywhere to this utopia of a forgotten world. As the excitement grew, he was standing up on the hump on the floor board of the old 39 ford in the back seat looking ahead to the right and back ahead. He kept saying, "Daddy are we almost there?" Theo would say, "not quite Tommy, just a little further."

Suddenly out of no where a beautiful doe and two fawns darted in front of the car. Theo slammed on the brakes as they jumped in the air and across the road, like they had wings. They disappeared into the thicket as quickly as they had appeared. Ahead Tommy could see a creek. His daddy headed straight for it. With the windows rolled down Tommy looked out of the window and down into the creek as his father drove right through the water. Oh! What fun! The creek was crystal clear as the big tires rolled on across to the other side. Immediately Tommy wanted to know if they were going to go through another. His daddy started laughing and said, "Yes, one More!"

Waiting with great anticipation, Tommy couldn't stand still, His eyes peeled to the road ahead as he hung his head out the window. He just knew he could smell the water ahead. It was hard to enjoy the wilderness around him for thinking about another creek ahead. Would this one be deep and would the water flood into the car? He wondered if his daddy knew. Whatever happened this six-foot four-inch giant of a man could protect he and his mom. Tommy never was afraid of anything as long as he had his dad around.

Before he knew it there out of the deep woods appeared a wonderful sight, a fast-flowing rocky stream. Tommy shouted, "Here we go!" The car bumped its way along across the rocks and swift current. Of course, the stream was only six or seven inches deep.

Theo, by now was getting into the fun Tommy was having. "Oh, I hope we can make it! I hope we don't float away! Oh, boy it is getting deep! Watch out for us Tommy, tell me if it looks like it is too deep." Tommy hung out the window trying his best to judge how deep it was. The sand was getting stirred up so he couldn't tell. Finally, all was well, as the car drove on dry land. "That was a close one Daddy." Tommy said.

What adventures lay ahead as a thousand thoughts ran through Tommy's mind. He knew he would love his Grandma Annie and her children, his aunts and uncle. The old shack was pretty shabby, but to a kid it was heaven!

Finally, in the clearing ahead the old house could be seen. Grannie's house, a garden, then Uncle Norris' house on the side of the hill. Grandma Annie had four daughters at home and one son. All the older men had died, including great grandpa Thomas Payne Strickland.

How strange to think of originally nine people lived in that little two room cabin. However, small as it was, happiness filled every square inch of its space. Good times and lean times, it was all a part of the cycle of life in the Valley of Shinbone and the Appalachian Mountains. This place they called home since the mid 1800's.

Doris Strickland Harwell and Tommy Wayne Harwell; 1947 in front of Annie's house in Shinbone Valley.

Finally arriving at Grandma's house Tommy leaped out of the back seat and into the front yard. Dust flying! He immediately took off his Keds and threw them on the porch. He felt the warm dirt between his toes as he ran to greet everyone. By the time the car stopped they were already standing out front waiting. Mary, Anne, Shirley, Joanne and Norris. Doris was the oldest sister of the eight children, Shelly, Inez and Norris were married at this time in 1947. The other girls were not of marrying age.

The first days were filled with wonder. Running down to the rocky stream, stumping his toes on stones along the way. He always seemed to have stumped toes in the summer. His Uncle Norris trying to keep up with Tommy, of course, he couldn't, he was fast as a jack rabbit. Down at the stream, he fell down on his stomach to get a closer look at the crawdads swimming in the crystal-clear water. He tried to catch some, but they were fast. Scooping up the water in his little fat hands.

With his fat fingers, he scooped up and drank the fresh spring water. It went down so cold it almost strangled Tommy. He then asked Norris where the water came from. Norris said, "come on up har with me and I'll shu ya." Tommy looked at him strangely and said "Ok." So, they climbed a little hill, that was steep and covered in beautiful rocks. Some were slick and smooth and had marks all threw them, while others were rough and jagged. At the top of the hill was a large area of rock, in the middle of it water was flowing out, like a small waterfall. Tommy was thrilled at the site of it. A small pool had formed at the bottom. Norris said this is where we get our dranking and cookin water, 'fresh out of them rocks.' If you dipped it down at the stream it could have trash in it. That water down thar is used for bathin and washin clothes. Tommy understood that because he saw that when he drank from it. Tommy asked if it ever turned off. Norris laughed and said, "sometimes it flowed less and sometimes it flowed more, but it never turned off."

Tommy was much older before he figured that out. Norris also said that the outhouse was "a piece" from where they washed. Tommy, of course, wanted to know why? Tommy was puzzled about that until later.

Tommy's mama and daddy would spend the night at Norris' and then head home at day break.

All of the young ones including Tommy, played in the yard around the small cabin, till well after dark. The grown-ups sat on the porch in rockers, straight chairs and anywhere they could and talked about whatever was the current news. Once it was dark the children got mason jars and caught firefly's, lighten bugs they called them. They caught frogs, them let them go before going into supper. Supper was at the big table in the cooking room. The fireplace lite the room up almost good enough to see, but they had a kerosene lamp on the table, so you wouldn't eat a bug in your food. Everyone had to wash-up before eating in a bucket on the porch. The soap was lye soap and it smelled strong, so the young'uns told Tommy to not use much. Tommy remembers the food tasting mighty good. Fried chicken freshly killed that day. Fresh greens with roots, corn on the cob, baked sweet potatoes and corn bread. The meal was a little special since Doris and Theo were there. Normally they didn't get chicken except on Sunday.

After supper the children sat on the floor in front of the big fire in the fireplace in the main room. The grownups sat around in chairs, Grandma Annie in her rocker.

Norris was a great story teller, so he told everyone that wanted to listen stories. Storytelling was handed down through the families. One designated person was always gifted with that special talent. A good storyteller could keep one on edge until the very end. Norris had that ability. I think the family knew he would have it because he was born with a crippled arm. That set him apart from the others. Tommy thought the world of Norris. He was humble and kind and always took time for him when he came to visit. He taught him a lot of the country ways.

Everything in Shinbone Valley was different from life in town. Just the fact they had no electricity, running water, indoor toilet, gas or electric heat. Not to count a radio or telephone.

Their life for all practical purposes was the same as it had been in the days of their great grandfather, Ancel Butler Strickland, in the mid 1800's.

After the wonderful stories they all went to bed. Everyone rose at day break, Tommy always slept in a big feather bed with four girls. It being the only bed except Grandma Annie's cot. No one got cold in the winter, that's for sure. Despite the cracks in the boards on the floors and walls, where the cold whistled through.

That big ole fireplace seemed to magically always have a roaring fire in it, if it was the least bit cold. Speaking of fires, Norris taught Tommy how to chip kindling. He loved the smell of the lighter wood they found in old tree stumps in the woods. It amazed him how an old dead stump, still provided an important use.

Norris showed him how to find sassafras. His grandma Annie loved to make tea out of it. One had to know how to use it because it could be poisonous. It was known to cure gout, arthritis, insect bites, eye swelling and several other ailments. The older folks seemed to know how to use things in nature. I believe they learned much from the Indians that were there when they arrived.

Natural Springs coming out of the rocks pooling at the bottom

CHAPTER VII
THE ROLLING STORE AND CHORES

Once a month a "Rolling Store" came through their way. It was at one time a large wagon, like a covered wagon, but in Tommy's youth, it was an old school bus. It stopped at every homestead in the area. Loaded down with things they couldn't make or grow, it was a big deal when they heard him coming down the road.

Grandma Annie may have gotten a new cooking pot or frying pan. A sack of flour, real coffee, a spoon for cooking and some needles for sewing. They didn't buy sugar. That white stuff just didn't taste as good as honey and maple syrup. Or as good as homemade sorghum. The children were always able to get a peppermint stick or licorice. Tommy remembers the excitement of the "Rolling Store" coming to Shinbone.

Speaking of meals earlier, breakfast was always special to Tommy. His Grandma made cathead biscuits with sorghum syrup, eggs, grits, salt pork or sometimes sausage. Those huge biscuits he never forgot. They were called cathead, because they were as big as a cat's head. People generally ate a big breakfast because they worked so hard, they needed a good start for the day.

Tommy did his share of work on his visits, however, he thought of it as play, because he enjoyed everything, they did every day.

He did get stuck in a vine once while picking muscadines high up in a tree. The girls were with him then and they had to get help from Norris after the tree broke and he fell out. He recalled thinking he was dying. He remembered sitting in a watermelon patch on the side of a hill and eating until he got sick. That wasn't as much fun as it started out.

Picking peaches, pears and figs early before the birds got to them was okay, but not his favorite thing to do. He preferred helping Norris. He thought he was grown up when he could do what Norris did.

Rolling Store, L-R: 213A1 Grover Whitener and 285A5 Marvin Kephart. Grover brought his wheelborrow to assist in the final delivery of purchases to his residence.

Norris taught Tommy how to plow, however that wasn't as easy as Norris made it look. Keeping the mule and plow straight on a surface that had stones everywhere, made for a difficult task for a boy of nine. Tommy would look over at Norris and see him bent over double laughing. As the summers passed and came again, Tommy grew strong and could do a man's work at eleven.

Nighttime was peaceful when Tommy was in that big feather bed all cozy and soft. When the lantern was blown out by the oldest girl, suddenly it was so dark, you couldn't see your hand in front of your face. This was something Tommy wasn't used to. In town there were street lights on every corner, which made for enough light after the light switch was turned off, to be able to see almost everything in his little room at home. In Shinbone, when it was dark outside, it was blackness inside. If it was a full moon, of course, the light would stream in across the floor and the bed and one could see the room and objects scattered about. The night sounds in the valley were louder than in town. The locus making their noise was a sweet sound along with the crickets and frogs croaking. Tommy loved to hear that as it lulled him to sleep.

Believed to be the last standing house near Ancel Butler Strickland's home site and land very near to where Chief Shinbone spent his last years.

On a stormy night the sound of the rain on the tin roof was like music to his ears as it danced with each pita pat. Then the lightening and thunder would roar and rumble and flash across the night sky, lighting up the whole place through the window next to the bed.

Sometimes on a quiet night one could hear the wolves howling in the distance, maybe on the ridge above the cabin. Occasionally the screaming sound of a panther would break the stillness of the night and make Tommy sit up in bed to listen more intently. Grannie always said it sounded like a woman screaming and it did. The woods were full of wild creatures and the night always brought them out.

The hoot-hoot of an ole owl in the big oak tree in the front yard, was a sound Tommy liked, as he lay there waiting to fall asleep. It was most certainly different than the sounds at night at home. There he listened for the twelve o'clock whistle of the east bound train coming through. Maybe, a neighbor's dog barking and a cat squalling as another ole tom cat chased it. That was the sounds of town at night. The deep woods and valleys of Shinbone were, it seemed, a million miles away.

If there was a fire still burning in the fireplace, one could see the orange glow filling the room with a soft dim light.

Tommy remembers going by the smoke house when he was outside. The smells coming form inside smelled so wonderful. The combination of hickory and hams, sausage, bacon and such was something one never forgets. Every time Grannie went in there for meat, Tommy wanted to go help. Just to get a better whiff of that aroma of sweet hickory smoked meat.

Mountain life had many pleasant memories, such as everything one ate was fresh from the land that it was raised and grew on. Something no one can claim today that lives in the city.

Canning was essential to preserve fruits and vegetables. Most folks had some kind of root cellar or dug out pit that was covered or even a small cave in the rock for keeping their preserves, vegetables, potatoes and such.

The mama cow usually didn't want to be still for her tits to be squeezed, but Tommy had learned to sweet talk her into standing real steal for his fingers to gently milk her ninnies. She gave enough for the house with plenty left for her pretty calf standing close by. Tommy gave the baby a big hug each morning. Mama cow seemed to like that as she rolled her big brown eyes at Tommy and mooed.

Tommy carefully carried the bucket full of milk, trying his best not to spill any, into grannie, that was waiting on him so she could make those wonderful biscuits he so loved. He has never forgotten them.

Everyone had chores before breakfast. Tommy and the girls had to take a bucket to the spring to get water for the day. Then they slopped the hogs, milked the cow, which was Tommy's job, while the girls feed the cow and mule. They next gathered eggs for breakfast. Then Grannie would make that wonderful breakfast that Tommy looked forward to each day. After breakfast Tommy had to churn the milk into butter. Not his favorite thing. The girls were making beds, cleaning the house, then swept the yard. Brooms were made from broom sage, a plant that looked similar to wheat in the field. It grew on unused land. Grass wasn't allowed to grow in yards. They were always swept clean. Washing was done on Saturday, outside in a large galvanized tub. It took two tubs to do the job, one for scrubbing with the wash board and the other for rinsing, before hanging on the clothes line. Grandma did that job with help from the oldest girl.

Baths were generally taken in the stream, except in cold weather, it was in the cabin in the washtub; in front of the fireplace. A nap usually followed for the little ones.

A good place for a swim or bath in the summer

TRIP TO PYRITON

Real civilization was only 25 miles from the valley. All the modern amenities of the 1940-50's. None the less, life in the valley was interwoven in their soul. The thoughts of complicating their lives with modern ways just didn't appeal to them. So, they stayed close to home and the little villages nearby. So, a trip was a big deal.

While staying in Shinbone Valley, Tommy got to experience the excitement of a day long trip to Pyriton by wagon.

Grandma Annie didn't own an automobile, in fact, no one anywhere near their place did. That being said, if one needed something in the nearest town, they traveled by mule and wagon. The children all got excited knowing they would get some candy from the general mercantile store. Grannie had corn that needed to be ground at the gristmill in town. I didn't mention it earlier, but few folks had money. Most everything was sold and bought by bartering. Grannie got her corn ground and paid for it with some of her corn. Also taking different items grown on the farm to trade for things that can't be grown on a small farm at the mercantile store. Grannie did spin wool for blankets and sweaters. Made dresses from flour sacks, cornmeal sacks also made good pillows. For some special occasions fabric by the yard was nice. She took her delicious jams and jellies, eggs and butter to trade. The owner was always glad to see her coming. Not many could match her jams.

The little girls had their noses pressed to the candy case trying to decide what they wanted. Tommy had his own money for candy and enough for an extra piece for the girls. Town was a real treat for all. Each time they went more and more people would be on the streets walking or riding. Several automobiles were driving down the streets as well.

The trip to Pyriton took all day as it was fifteen miles from Shinbone. On a mule drawn wagon it took quite awhile crossing streams along the way. No bridges were built at that time. Eating a lunch prepared ahead of time to eat on the way, there and back. Cold fried chicken, boiled eggs and biscuits was mighty good to all of them.

Stopping in the rock bottomed stream to let the mule drink gave the young'uns time to go to the woods for relief. Being careful not to squat over a snake, since the woods were full of venomous ones. If bitten, some were deadly to the victim. Moccasins and rattlesnakes mostly.

As the sun was setting behind the mountains, the girls and tommy were tuckered out. By the time home was reached it was dark and all was quiet in the back of the wagon.

Annie, Norris and his wife Ester were riding up front. Norris hollered, "Get out young'uns, we're home."

Everyone jumped out and ran in the house ready for bed.

Sometimes nighttime was for more interesting pursuits. Norris asked Tommy if he wanted to go possum hunting. Well, of course, he did.

In the Old Days

Loaded with the dogs, guns, a lantern and courage off they went. The woods were dark and scary for a little boy. They walked for quite awhile till the dogs got a scent and started running. Finally, Norris held the lantern up to a tall tree and eyes peered back at them. Norris shot several times at the hole in the tree until a couple of possums fell out. Norris put them in a croaker sack and went on as the dogs had another possum scent ahead. They repeated the same thing. With two sacks full of possums they made their way home in the dark.

They put the sacks of possums on the porch. Tommy remembered being so pleased with himself, knowing he was now a hunter. However, he couldn't sleep, so he went out on the porch to check on their prize. To Tommy's surprise, the sacks were laying there empty!

Next morning Norris came over and saw the possum tracks leading away from the house. He told Tommy, "That's way they call em possums, they play dead." He laughed and laughed about that. Tommy thought about that for some time, before he realized the joke was on him. He learned a good lesson, He never went possum hunting again.

CHAPTER VIII
THE STORY TELLER

In the evenings after supper and before bedtime, everyone would sit around the large stone fireplace and watch the fire and its dancing flames and the burning embers falling in the ashes with a popping sound. One had to be watchful that one didn't pop out on the person nearest it. The warmth of the fire gave them that feeling of peace and comfort. The flames almost hypnotizing to the point of making one spellbound as they stared into the fire. This of course caused a silence to fall on all the children and the sandman was soon to follow.

On the nights of Norris' storytelling, the children got as close to him as possible to be sure they didn't miss a word. His tales of ghostly encounters were especially interesting. The creepy old man story that was half eaten by a bear and wouldn't die. He wandered aimlessly in the forest on cold winter nights, crying out for someone to save him. Appearing out of the darkness with his flesh torn from his body. One arm dangling to the side, half eaten. He would holler out, "Help Me!", then as soon as a settler saw him, he would disappear in a misty vapor. "Many had seen him," Norris said. The children began clinging to one another in a state of fear and excitement. "Tell another one, Norris" they shouted. Usually one story at a time was enough to give them all nightmares that night. That big feather bed was a safe haven, as they snuggled up together almost disappearing in the overstuffed bed of goose feathers.

Just before they fell asleep, they listened intently for any sound of the half eaten old man crying out in the darkness of the night. Every little sound made them shiver. Then quiet and sleep fell on all the occupants of that big ole soft bed. Home made quilts piled high up to their necks and sometimes over their heads. Such memories as those go through Tom's mind now, as he goes back to the valley in his thoughts. Old men seem to do that in their senior years. They want to talk over and over about those special memories as a child.

Sundays were special in Shinbone Valley. Grandma Annie cooked the largest meal of the week. To start with if Norris had killed enough rabbits the night before, that was the meat. Fried in lard and then making the gravy from the drippins. Everyone loved fried rabbit. Her wonderful melt in your mouth buttered cat head biscuits, fresh picked turnips with roots, purple hull peas, fried cut okra, corn on the cob with fresh butter, cabbage, new boiled red potatoes, and candied yams for desert. Fresh churned buttermilk brought from the spring to keep it cold. That was a typical Sunday dinner.

Sometimes Annie and her bunch went to dinner on the ground at Union Church on Sunday. Everyone showed up for these occasions with all the women bringing their best cooked dishes. Every kind of meat from hams to possums. Fresh vegetables of every kind grown in the valley. Jams and jellies, pies and cakes, apple turnovers, buttermilk, tea, cider and sometimes mulberry wine on the side. Children played, ladies gossiped, men played games, and all enjoyed the music at the end of the day. Some gospel and some ole time Appalachian music.

Instruments like banjos, fiddles, guitar, and dulcimer were the most popular. Much of this music came with them from Scotland. Some folks would really get into the spirit of the music and dance. The children really enjoyed dancing.

These functions lasted all day and lanterns had to be used to see their way home once the sun set and darkness was upon them.

The people of the valley looked out for one another in times of sickness and trouble. If a barn caught fire, it could be seen for miles in the sky. Neighbors came from all around to help put it out and get the livestock out safe, if possible. Sometimes it was too late.

Norris got together with the men who lived within a few miles and they had a little party of their own. Tommy was witness to a few of these get togethers. The men were drinking something that looked like water out of mason jars. Soon it was obvious it wasn't water. Tommy, seeing his father intoxicated he recognized the effect of alcohol. They were telling stories and the more they drank the more outrageous the stories got. Then the arguing began. One was a better hunter than the other; one was stronger than the other. Next, they settled that with arm wrestling. Norris, even with one crippled arm, was about the strongest one there.

Typical Church of that time

Tommy watched all of this unfold thinking they acted like he and his friends back home. Foolish! After all the moonshine was gone the men were pretty much in the same shape, foolish and drunk. Somehow, they made their way home in the dark of night, unless they passed out on the way home. The horses probably had more sense at that point and got them there.

Luckily this wasn't done on a regular basis. Besides, moonshine was illegal. One could go to jail if caught.

Cheaha Mountain was the vista in front of Grandma Annie's cabin. All one had to do was look up. The home of the Strickland's was at the very bottom of valley of the mountain.

Cheaha being the highest point in the state of Alabama. The valley was lovely to look at, with meadows, forests and babbling brooks and streams, all coming from spring heads scattered all along the mountain side. A place of beauty that only seeing in person can truly give one the real sense of its majesty. When the sun set over the mountains it was a thing of immeasurable splendor. The sun rising in the valley was a lovely site, as the mist seemed to rise with the morning sun. Certain times, a blue mist would and will settle on the mountains in a ghostly veil. A site that has to be seen with one's own eyes to take in the magic. The Cherokee Indians called it "Shaconage", a place of blue smoke.

How fortunate to be born in such a place as this. The closest thing to heaven on earth. The way God made it.

There had been a covered bridge many years before but got washed away

This drawing and a couple of the others were drawn by my brother, Randal Knight from Ellisville, Mississippi.

CHAPTER IX
THE LAST VISIT TO SHINBONE VALLEY

The last summer at Shinbone Valley for Tommy was when he was twelve. He learned the area so well by that time, that he ventured out on this own many days after chores. The woods were very close by. A day in the woods was one of great enjoyment for a boy of twelve. The forest was so thick that very little under growth grew. Tommy could walk and explore with no trouble with briars and bushes. He would come to springs all through the woods where rocks and marble were scattered about. He would pick up beautiful stones and pieces of marble, not really realizing what they were. He would find Indian artifacts near the springs. Broken pottery, hollowed out stone, arrow heads and beads. Never really thinking of collecting any of those ancient relics, he looked at them and just threw them down where he found them. They were so common on his walks, that he didn't know the real significance of what he found. Of course, now he wished he had kept all of them.

Tommy remembers huge rocks and slabs of marble, granite and slate. Not to count the glorious virgin timber towering to the sky. A shear heaven for any child that loved nature.

Tommy picked wild blueberries or huckle berries, blackberries and wild plums on his walks. He knew to be careful of snakes, especially near blackberries. If he got tired, he would just sit down by a big tree and rest. The ground was covered in pine straw and pine cones.

As Tommy sat, leaned against the tree, little critters would come around. Rabbits and squirrels never realizing he was even there. He watched them scamper about. The squirrels were eating the new fallen pine cones and acorns all over the ground. Also gathering them to take to their nests in the tall trees. The rabbits were eating sprigs of fresh grass coming up through the pine straw. Sometimes he spotted a deer in the distance eating berries off the huckleberry bushes.

Heading home he saw another deer drinking from one of the springs as he grew closer, he leaped over the rocks so graceful and easy and was out of site.

Tommy had no idea that the summer of 1952 would be his last visit to Shinbone Valley, in his youth. This year a trip is planned to return to this place of cherished memories.

His Grandma Annie left with a gold prospector that year, never to return. The youngest child, Shirley, moved in with one of her married sisters.

The old cabin was abandoned and surely rotted down by now, with nature reclaiming the homestead and out buildings.

All of his adopted family of that generation are all gone now.

Woods in Shinbone Valley

ANNISTON

On one of Tommy's many adventures in the great forest near home in Anniston, he came across graves of POW's from WW II. He wasn't aware of who they were until he was told. They were graves of German prisoners of war.

Fort McClellan had an encampment during the war, and this was where they were buried. Fort McClellan was not very far from Tommy's home in Anniston. During WWII, it was one of the largest army forts in the U.S. and it closed in 1999. About 16,000 German POW's were imprisoned there. Twenty-six German had died and were buried there, but it was considered a model prison camp. Even the Germans spoke well of it.

Tommy spent quite a bit of time alone roaming the woods during the weekends. He had friends but they didn't have the same interest Tommy had, so he did his own thing. That entailed walking for miles into the deep woods all day, then coming out in the late afternoon. Just being around nature made him feel fulfilled inside. That might sound strange for a young boy of ten or so, but it is what he felt. He knew he was different some how from his parents and later his sister and brother.

Tommy loved going to the picture shows in town. He always went alone and always on Saturdays. He walked to town about three miles from home. The theater he went to was called the Ritz Theater, which was one of three in town. He would stay all day in the theater watching the double features and the serials shown in between each movie. *Gene Autry, Hop along Cassidy, The Lone Ranger, Roy Rogers and Zorro*, were the serials that played in those days when Tommy was a boy. He loved anything with Indians. He was about ten to twelve years old. It was dark when he walked home.

Doris and Theo didn't attend church when Tommy was growing up. However, Tommy talked about his desire to go with his daddy. Some of Tommy's friends attended church and talked about the Bible stories in Sunday school they learned. He loved hearing about them. After telling his daddy, Theo, would walk Tommy to the Presbyterian Church not far from home and lift him up to the church window and inside, where his friends waited. He did this often, so his boy could learn about Jesus, unlike his background of never getting that opportunity as a child.

When Tommy was older about fourteen, he joined the Noble Street Baptist Church. Later he joined the Golden Springs Baptist Church as an adult.

At night as a child, Tommy and neighborhood children would sit outside the Pentecostal Church and listen to the music. He loved how enthusiastic the music and sermon were.

Being in school during the day while his mother and father worked. His afternoons were alone at home after he didn't need a Mamie anymore. He missed her and wished she could still be there. His memories of her are sweet and dear to him.

Tommy would play outside and all over the neighborhood until dark. When he went home and walked in the door, he could smell his Mama's cooking. She was a good cook and seemed to cook a lot of recipes in a pressure cooker. His favorite dishes were her roast with all the trimmings, of course, she made wonderful biscuits and cornbread. Her fried chicken was pretty tasty too. One of Tommy's favorite desserts was her fruit turnovers, made from fresh apples, pears and peaches. An unforgettable peach tree was at the back door.

Tommy had neighborhood friends and school friends that he ran the streets with on the weekends. They played football in the open fields nearby. He did the normal things a young boy did. Climbed trees, explored abandoned buildings, built forts and played war games. When they played cowboys and Indians, Tommy always wanted to be an Indian. When picking a toy in a store he would pick a war bonnet and bow and arrows. He couldn't escape what was in his genes.

We know his mother's maternal and paternal grandparents were supposedly Cherokee Indian, or at least half. His mother, Naomi, looked Indian in her pictures. Tommy looked very much like her, except much more handsome. Trying to search his ancestry has been interesting.

Going back a little, when Tommy was really young, about four, WWII was raging in Europe and the Pacific. Fort McClellen was overflowing and the lack of accommodations for soldiers and spouses. Therefore, folks in the surrounding area had opened their homes to GI's and wives. Everyone in America did their part to help the war effort. Even though Doris and Theo's home was very small they took in a young soldier and his new bride.

On one particular occasion Doris had come in from work and prepared a good meal for everyone. She was tired and it was not one of her best days. As everyone sat down to eat in the tiny kitchen, conversations began. Right in the middle of this, the soldier's wife said something very rude about Doris' potato salad not being fit to eat! Well…that was a big mistake! Doris got up and walked around the table to where this young woman was sitting. Without a word, she dumped the whole bowl on her head! She then said, "See if that fits!"

You didn't want to mess with a red head! I believe they found another place to stay.

When Tommy was about thirteen, Doris' sister came to live with them. Inez was Tommy's favorite Aunt and she always made time for him as a boy. She was a pretty girl too, and from Tommy's account was as sweet as she was pretty. She lived there close to a year, with no place else to go. She knew her big sister would take her in. Doris was like that about her family.

Inez met a nice young man while living there. They married and moved to a nearby town.

Mary and Jo Anne lived there for a few months too. After their mother ran off with a gold prospector. Annie had some good qualities, however when it came to men, she was nonsensical and pretty much thoughtless of others. She left several children with no place to go.

The girls eventually found work and a place of their own until each found love and married.

Doris could be a mean woman at times, but also a good person who dearly loved her kin folk.

Tommy(Tom) is grateful for her love and choosing to adopt him. His life could have been so much worse if not for her compassion.

CHAPTER X
TOM GROWN UP

Tommy grew into a young man, graduating from high school in Anniston. He had played football in school and was good. He was strong for his height and weight.

No longer called Tommy, just Tom, he decided to join the Marines. It didn't take long for him to be playing football in the Marines. He grew stronger and his weight picked up. Everything was going well when the Cold War talks with Russia threatened to be war with the Communist Cuban Castro. John F. Kennedy was President at the time. The American fleet was shipped out to Cuba. It seems the Soviet Union was building missile sites in Cuba. The whole objective was to have the power to strike America from the Caribbean with nuclear attack. It was more a ploy to bolster the Soviet Unions bargaining power, but still a good possibility of nuclear war. American blocked the whole island and had planned to overthrow Castro, with a Cuban Army that had escaped Cuba earlier. Their attack failed. However, Kennedy and Nikita Khrushchev, settled the possible war and very possibly saved the world. The Cuban crisis has been referred to as "The Bay of Pigs." Tom was out on a ship circling Cuba and waiting for instructions. Thankfully the Russian roulette ended! "The Week the World Stood Still." Never has America been so close to nuclear destruction along with the whole world. The year was 1961.

After the Marines, Tom was offered a college football scholarship at a very good college. Sadly, he had to refuse because his father had become a complete invalid and his mother had divorced him, and he had no one to take care of him. Tom went to college at night and worked days, never satisfied with where his life was taking him. After his father passed away, he decided to leave.

Finally, he went to Texas to train to be a mud engineer with an oil company. In 1974, while checking a rig in Mississippi he met the author of his book.

He had a very successful career as a Mud Engineer and went on to manage an Oil Company. Later he became a Mississippi PGA Club Pro and was a top golfer in the state. Running a golf course in Laurel, Mississippi.

Finally going into several business ventures with the Author, Marcelle and now in semi-retirement. Still together after forty-four years.

On being given away and adopted…

Tommy decided years ago to be satisfied with what God dealt him. To be happy with no bitterness in his heart towards anyone and be grateful for and love the only family he knew and that loved him even though he was not their blood kin. He was always treated the same by all of his adopted kin folks.

Thomas Wayne Harwell

The truth of his real father will never be known, if indeed, he ever was known. There is serious speculation in that matter.

Tom hardly thinks of it. He knows what kind of man he is and is not ashamed to admit he never knew his father. Personally, one of the things I most admired about him after first meeting him is that he is a man of integrity and honor, moral and good. He has a good loving heart and just wanted to be loved. Which apparently, he didn't have before in his life. My children, grandchildren and great grandson are considered his, in his love for them and they feel the same for him. He loves his children from his previous marriage and his grandchildren and great grandchildren. He feels blessed to leave a legacy of love behind when he is gone onto his eternal home.

Our new great grandson will carry on the Thomas name.

As for Shinbone Valley...

As a child Tommy has wonderful memories of that hidden valley. A place as close to God's creations as one can get.

Looking back, he now realizes it was a magical time in his life as a child. A place that can never be revisited like it was in his childhood. But the memories will linger as long as he remembers the sweetness of summer.

This is his story...

Thomas Wayne Harwell married Marcelle Bartran Holloway
March 8, 1975

Tom and Marcelle Harwell; 1980

Tom with his two daughters, Marlyn and Cathy, 2017

Tom's grandson Ryan Huff and wife Amy with their three girls, Eva Ryan, Laurel Pearl and Virginia Blair, 2018

Tom's daughter Cathy and granddaughter Sydney, 2018

Tom's Grandson Chase and Granddaughter Sydney

Tom and his adopter daughter, Lori Holloway Howell and beloved daughter in love, Carri Shoemake (Rest in Peace), 2017

Tom's Grandson, Benjamin Smith and girlfriend
Macy, 2017

Marcelle and Tom's daughter and granddaughter; Lori and Madelyn

Our Granddaughter's wedding; Madelyn and Zachary Jordan

Madelyn, Zachary and baby Thomas Jordan

Madelyn and Thomas

Marcelle, Tom and Thomas

Tom and Thomas

Our Son, Victor Holloway and Granddaughter Chelsea

Our Grandson, Pace Holloway

Our Grandson, Isaac Holloway; 1996-2015

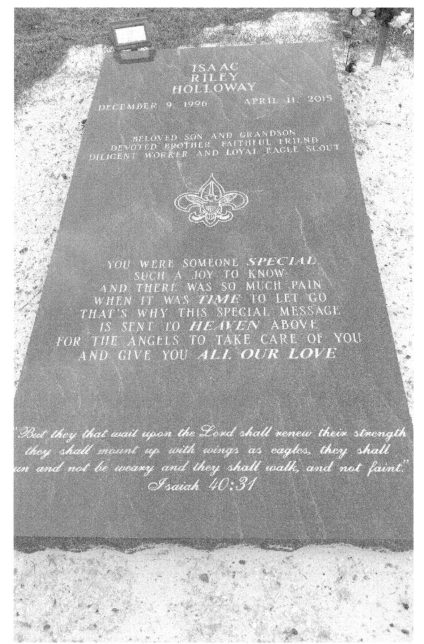

Our Grandson, Isaac Holloway; "Beloved by All"

Thomas and Marcelle Harwell

Made in United States
Orlando, FL
12 June 2024

47778241R00055